Rowing on the Snohomish

Rowing on the Snohomish

Bill Jaquette

ISBN-13: 9781545512463
ISBN-10: 1545512469
Library of Congress Control Number: 2017906552
CreateSpace Independent Publishing Platform
North Charleston, South Carolina

Foreword

I HAVE LONG KNOWN that exercise is one of the keys to health. For many years, I did what many people did: go running. But running for me was always just a task often done in the early-morning darkness, not infrequently in the rain, and sometimes on a path by an angry dog. My distaste often allowed me to find an excuse not to go. I had to find something better for me. I have been involved in boating all my life and knew how to row—rowing a small dinghy within an area of a couple hundred yards to go fishing or to meet up with another boat. However, I had never thought of it as something of worth in itself.

In my early days on the water sailing and fishing, I would see others out rowing in shells and like most people growing up in western Washington, I was well aware of the exploits of the University of Washington crew. But I had not given it a try myself until I entered law school and bought a single shell as a diversion from my studies. That time on the water and away from shore was the start of my progression to a full dedication to rowing, more precisely sculling, as a major part of my way of life.

Along the way, my focus on rowing has led me to build three wooden boats. The first was a cosine wherry. The book *Rip, Strip & Row,* by J. D. Brown, provided the plans and instructions for construction of a fourteen-foot rowing boat, designed by John Hartsock, that was built out of three-quarter-inch cedar strips. From that success and with the help of a number of boat-building classes, I built a seventeen-foot Whitehall of classic lapstrake construction (like the Viking ships) from a table of offsets I found in *Building Classic Small Craft, Volume 1,* by John Gardner. My pride and joy to this day, I have taken *Thurgood* on a number of rowing/camping trips in the San Juan Island in Washington and the Gulf Islands in British Columbia, Canada. The third boat, a true rowing shell, I built from plans that I created on a computer boat-design program. While a success in its own way, it was too heavy and was destroyed in trying to make it lighter.

Along the way, I discovered Sound Rowers, an organization that sponsors a number of regattas inviting any human-powered crafts—kayaks, canoes, peddle boats, and rowing boats of all kinds—to race on various open-water courses around western Washington. Over the years, I raced each of those boats that I built and the sculls I have purchased to succeed them in many of the Sound Rowers races. However, rowing didn't become the major part of my way of life until I joined the Everett Rowing Association and placed my shell in their boathouse on the Snohomish River, reducing the number of steps it takes to get launched.

Rowing is now the most significant thing I do for exercise. I row an average of three times per week, varying more or fewer based on the weather. Each outing lasts about an hour and a half. Unlike some people who enjoy exercise for its own sake, I need something more to inspire me into action. That is the job of the Snohomish River.

The book consists of four chapters, one for each season of the year. Each chapter contains stories of rowing on the Snohomish River in that season. The stories are based primarily on the events of a particular outing, but I have added some events from other outings to give a fuller picture of what I am experiencing.

Each season is different. Winter is the story of struggling with limited daylight, cold, windy, and wet weather, and the occasional rewards for my struggles to get out there. Much of the story of spring is about the revival of the trees and plants and the emergence of the birds and other animals, and the other rowers. Summer is a time for taking some longer expeditions along alternate waterways. On expeditions in the fall,

I experience the shortening of the day and the cooling temperatures, the return of the fog, the trees losing their leaves, and the birds settling down for winter or planning to fly south to avoid it. In every season I get to experience the trees along the shore with the mountains rising behind, the sky in all its varieties and their reflections in the calm waters of the river.

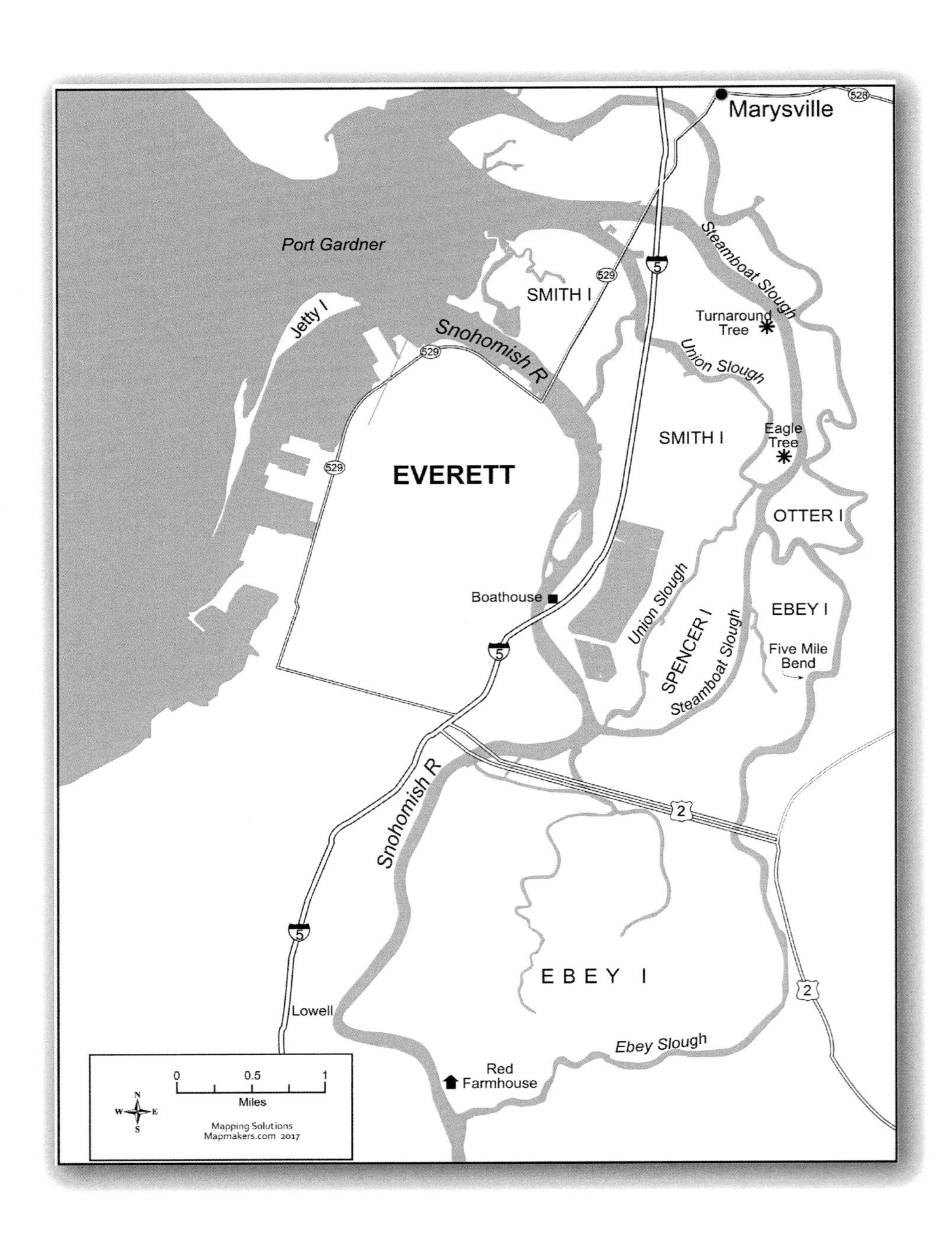

Marysville
528
Port Gardner
Steamboat Slough
5
529
SMITH I
Jetty I
Snohomish R
529
Turnaround Tree
Union Slough
SMITH I
Eagle Tree
529
EVERETT
OTTER I
Boathouse
Union Slough
SPENCER I
Steamboat Slough
EBEY I
Five Mile Bend
5
Snohomish R
2
5
EBEY I
2
Lowell
Ebey Slough
Red Farmhouse
0
0.5
1
Miles
N
W
E
S
Mapping Solutions
Mapmakers.com 2017

1

Winter

It is still dark, but I have to get to work, and winter is late with its morning light. I caught the morning weather on the TV, and it's going to be cold and cloudy, but the rain is not due until afternoon, and it's a definite time to go. This time of year, I won't be the first person to the Everett Rowing Association boathouse; the Morning Glory rowing group will be there for their 6:00 a.m. workout on the rowing machines. The sun will rise at 7:52, which, if I push it a bit, will allow me to hit the water at about 7:20 with enough light to be able to see where I am going. During the winter, I am going to be rowing my more-stable Maas 24 scull. She is named *Piper,* a name used for boats by three generations of my family. I always thought of it as a very nice woman's name but have recently figured out that the name might have come into use because my grandfather smoked a pipe.

It is cold enough that part of me is looking for an excuse to turn around and go home and get on the stair stepper in my warm house, but as usual, the effort to gather up my rowing gear and drive to the boathouse creates enough momentum that the other part of me wins the debate. I rig the boat and take the oars and water bottle to the dock. The part of the Snohomish River we row on is affected by tide, and the speed and direction of the current in the river vary substantially. It is still pretty dark, but in the reflection of some lights from across the river, I can see that there is a pretty strong current, and the flow is downstream. My row upstream is going to be a little slower, but if the tide doesn't change, it will be a quick trip home.

There is frost on the dock, and I have this vision of falling with the boat on top of me, so it is important to go slowly. All goes well. I lift the boat into the water, put in the oars, shift myself onboard, and shove off. Those first strokes feel a little awkward; have I forgotten how to do this? No, I just need to get the boat moving; it stabilizes, and I am away. It is still twilight, but the dim light of predawn and the reflections in the water make me happy to have gotten away and not be part of the roar of the traffic I hear on the bridge overhead.

Rowing a scull is a very efficient form of movement. The nine-and-a-half-foot oars provide great leverage for pulling against the water and the required stabilizing for the very slender and fast hull. The sliding seat allows me to add the power of the legs to that of the arms and back. It is exhilarating to be able to travel so swiftly and efficiently with such little disturbance of the water.

Piper

As I move upriver, it gets lighter and lighter, and the reflection in the water turns from blue to silver. The branches of trees begin to stand out clear against the gray sky. The seagulls resting in the river wait until the last second to move out of my way.

I have some choices where to go: stay on the river or head down Steamboat Slough. It is duck-hunting season, and you can often hear gunfire on the slough. But it's a weekday, and there won't be as many hunters out, so I decide to try the slough. Once I get past that old marina, the slough takes me out into nature. Although hidden in the clouds, the sun is now fully up. I can see the trees along the bank showing clearly in the water against the silver reflection of the gray sky.

Uh-oh, gunfire. I have never felt that I was down range from shots being fired, but it still makes me a little nervous. I carry a small air horn that I tape to the boat during hunting season; I give it three blasts to make sure that the hunters know I am here.

First Light of Day

There are always birds around. It is still early winter, and it seems as if they are mostly just hanging out, waiting for spring. Over there, I see a lone bald eagle perched high on a bare tree. A little later on, I see two others sitting next to one another, one looking out over the river toward the hills to the east. There seem to be more eagles around in the winter. Perhaps that is because they are more visible when the trees are bare; perhaps they are just hanging out and waiting for some food source to come back elsewhere. There goes another one flying far overhead and landing in the tree over there. Swimming along, up ahead I can see a pair of common mergansers, the male in black and white and the gray female with its red hood. They are smart not to be flying high this time of year.

I have named a number of locations on the river as places to turn around and head back. Today I row past Eagle Tree, named by me because it is the most reliable place to see eagles on my route on

Steamboat Slough. I used this as my turnaround objective for a number of years. I don't have any early appointments; I think I'll go to Turnaround Tree. Passing Eagle Tree and heading on to Turnaround Tree, it comes to mind that every stroke I row now means a longer trip and more strokes to get me back. So it is just a bit of relief to turn around and head back now with an idea of how much energy it is going to take.

Eagle Tree

Turnaround Tree

Out rowing by myself is a good time for thinking. Once the requirements for a powerful stroke and the necessities for keeping my balance passed from my conscious brain to my unconscious brain, rowing became a good time for thinking. The rhythmic use of the body's muscles producing that quiet and efficient movement through the water helps to keep what is going on in the conscious brain in balance too.

Thump, I hit a log. The momentum carries the boat up on top of it. The collision causes a knot in my left thigh muscle. Fortunately, it is not a large log, and the boat slides on over, only banging again when the log hits the skeg. As I knead the knot out of my muscle, I think back to a run-in with a much bigger log when the boat did not pass over but got stuck on top with my weight positioned right over the log, crushing the boat. I well remember the sound of the cracking fiberglass. I did make it back to the dock that day, filling with water as I went, but the boat had to go in for substantial repairs.

I have a mirror on my hat like bicyclists wear, which allows me to keep an eye forward, but the thinking I so enjoy distracted me from keeping watch. I remind myself to stay aware from here on. Good thing I remember that deadhead that planted itself just about here a couple of weeks ago. A deadhead is a floating tree with its root system sunk to the bottom and the top of its trunk at the surface of the water waiting to encounter an unwary boater. There it is. I pull over to the side of the river to pass.

I am getting close to home. Looking around, I see that the clouds have lifted a little. I can see the foothills to the east showing some fresh snow. Clouds still hide the mountains beyond; getting a look at them will have to wait for another day.

I'm moving fast now. The current in the main river makes it a quick part of the trip, and I pass the dock, make a U-turn, and pull up. I sit there for a moment, have a drink of water, take out the oars and climb out. Pulling the boat out of the water and hoisting it onto my shoulders is a significant exertion, a little tougher now because of the nine miles I have just rowed. Walking up the ramp with *Piper* on my shoulder focuses my eyes on a large white alder tree across the road at the top. It is now bare, but I anticipate the varying visions it will present to me over the course of the year. At the top, I put the boat on the slings and go back to the dock to retrieve the oars and my water bottle. It takes me a few minutes to wipe the boat down and put her back on her rack in the boathouse. Now I am off to work.

Welcoming Alder in Winter

⅄ ⅄ ⅄

In winter, I always look at the outdoor thermometer I have at my house before leaving for a row. For the last few days, it has been unusually cold, into the single digits. If other factors are favorable, I will row in the teens, but the single digits kept me onshore. Today looks doable, no wind and no rain. The temperature is in the high twenties, and it's Saturday, so I can wait until the sun is fully up.

I launch and head out but soon encounter something new to me, a patch of thin ice floating down the river. I pull to the side and easily avoid it. However, not far along, I encounter another, larger patch that I can't avoid. The ice is very thin, and *Piper* manages to move through without too much difficulty. The oars chop into the ice, which provides firmer than usual points to pull against, and I am soon back into fluid water.

There seem to be more sheets of ice flowing in my direction in the faster current in the main river, and I decide to head down Steamboat Slough. A few hundred yards down the slough, I see that this was a mistake. The calmer water in the slough has allowed the ice to form from one bank to the other. It is still thin, and I can chop my way along, but this isn't fun, and I turn around and head back.

Just as I reach the main river, an eagle swoops overhead within twenty feet; moments later, it does it again. I soon realize that it isn't me that the eagle is after; it's a duck swimming along about thirty feet behind me. The winter months have forced the eagles away from their normal fish diet to other sources of food. As the eagle swoops down, the duck dives under the water to avoid the attack. When the duck surfaces, the eagle swoops in again. I am afraid that the duck is going to become exhausted from the continual diving and, forced to remain at the surface to catch an extra breath, will get caught in the eagle's attack. Perhaps disturbed by my presence, and fortunately for the duck, the eagle gives up and flies off to a nearby light pole.

To make up for the row I was missing, I rowed a ways downriver past the dock. Here, the river water mixes with the saltwater in Port Gardner Bay, and ice is not a problem. I row a couple of miles down to the industrial sites along the river, turn around, and head back. I am going to remember that strategy the next time I encounter ice.

It rains a lot in the wintertime in the Northwest. In Seattle on average, it rains on more days than it doesn't from November through March. However, rainy fronts often pass through in short order, leaving plenty of opportunities for a dry row. Every now and again, however, you just have to row in the rain. After all, it is just water. Well, today is one of those days. The forecast the night before offered hope of a little break, but the early-morning TV meteorologist let me know that the front had come in early. Any chance of talking myself out of going disappeared when I saw that the Everett Rowing Club had put together a group of hearty master rowers for a morning row. At least it is calm. As I launch, I can see the rain hitting the water. Most of

Masters Rowers Launching

the drops hit the water like tiny pebbles, but occasionally drops will roll around the surface for a brief moment like a tiny, clear marble.

It is a weekend, and I can hear the hunters, so I decide to stay in the river and row up past the city of Everett's river harbor. Shortly after leaving the dock, I meet the other rowers. They have turned around and are headed back to the warm and dry of the clubhouse. The low clouds and the insistent rain make me feel a bit lonely. It is heartening to see three large harbor seals lying up on a rotting log boom. They turn and lift up their heads just enough to watch me row past. An eagle sitting on a tree behind them sees something in the water, swoops down, and grabs a hold of it. It starts to lift it out of the water, but whatever that was is too heavy, and the eagle is forced to let go and fly back to its perch in the tree.

Harbor Seal Getting Out of the Cold Water

Once past the harbor, there is farmland to the east. On the other side of the river, I see the blue tarps and other gear of the several homeless encampments. My time out in the wet and cold will be over in an hour. That allows me to find pleasure and satisfaction being out here. I cannot imagine how it would be to have no escape.

We had some heavy rains over the last few days, and the river has been pretty full. That means that there are probably some logs to watch out for. There is one now right in the middle of the river. It looks pretty fresh; the limbs are gone, but the root system rises out of the water menacingly. I row far over to the side of the river to pass it. I need to remember this guy when I head back down river. You can encounter all sorts of floating hazards on the Snohomish River. There are some old logs that have been around for a while. I am guessing that they had spent time washed up onshore, but the rising water level has launched them once again to float up and down stream with the incoming and outgoing tides until coming ashore when the rain lets up and the river returns to its normal levels.

I have made it to the sharp bend in the river at the community of Lowell and now turn around and head back. The rain hasn't let up, and I am pretty wet. The evaporation of the water, even on the outside of my raincoat, is cooling me off. So it is time to finish the row. Fortunately, I am now traveling with the current and moving along nicely. I pass that log, which has kindly floated over to one side of the river. Before long, I am back at the dock. As I carry my boat up the ramp, I can see, as I suspected, that mine is the only car left in the lot. In order to get my boat dry, I have to set up slings inside the boathouse. No reason to hang around. I put things away and drive home, remembering to sit on a plastic bag to keep the car's seat dry.

Homeless Camp

⅄⅄⅄

Every now and again during winter, you get one of those days—clear, cold, and calm. This is one of those days. It is well below freezing—time to dress in my warmest outfit, bring that extra heavy vest, and be sure to wear the beanie under my hat. As I drive to the boathouse, I can see, against the barely lit sky, the dark shapes of the mountains to the east, Whitehorse and Three Fingers standing out over the rest. The temperature of the air is twenty-one degrees, which is just about half the temperature of the water in the river. There is frost all over, so it is important to walk carefully while carrying *Piper* and, particularly, to remember to take baby steps when I get to the slippery dock. As I put *Piper* into the water, a bird flies up and lands on one of the nearby pilings. In this very early-morning light, I can only see its shape, but I can tell that it is some kind of a hawk. It gives me a quick look and flies away. I climb aboard, and I, too, am away.

It hasn't rained much in the last couple of days, and the cold temperature means that the snow is staying in the mountains, so the current isn't particularly strong. I need to stay alert for the logs that have been moving up and down the river with the changing currents, and I am sure that the high tide will have lifted those two deadheads and moved them to rest somewhere new. However, the visibility is good, and the rising sun is making it better every minute, so navigation isn't going to be a problem.

Eagle on Frosty Tree

I have the cold pretty well under control except for my hands. My light bike gloves do nothing to keep my hands warm, and the pulling on the oars inhibits the flow of warming blood into my fingers. It is going to take a while, but eventually the capillaries in my hands will expand from the increasing blood pressure of my exercise, and I will begin to feel a burning in my fingers as they begin to get warm.

With the full sun, everything brightens. Every branch of the leafless alder trees, even the smallest twig, is covered with frost glowing bright white against the blue sky, all reflecting in the calm river. It brightens my mood, and it looks to have done the same for the eagle perched proudly on the high branch of that tree. The hunting season is over, so it is safe to head down Steamboat Slough, and there are more eagles and even one hawk to be seen. Heading down the slough, I can see Mount Olympus and the rest of the Olympic range, only to see it disappear as I pass the next bend in the river. As the river turns, Mount Rainier briefly appears in the distance. Winter is the best time for mountain viewing; there is more snow, and there is not the haze that you see in the summer.

Well, here I am at Turnaround Tree. Time to turn around. I dig the port oar into the water, and the boat begins to pivot around. Ten strokes with my starboard oar complete the turn, and I am headed back. As I row back up the slough, I can see Mount Baker behind me to the north, a brilliant white in the sun. One of the ever-present harbor seals pops its head out of the water, gives me a quick glance, and moves on. The rowing has been uneventful, and it will continue to be if I remember to stay to the right when passing that deadhead about half of the way back to the main river.

When the sun is fully up and the course of the river permits, I like to put myself in line with the reflection of the sun on the water. The disturbance in the water in my wake scatters the reflection of the sun and gives me a glowing trail as I row.

Piper with a Trail of Reflecting Sunlight

Once in the main river, it is a quick trip with the current back to the boathouse. On landing, I notice that the water that splashed upon deck during my row has frozen, and there are icicles hanging from the gunnels, testimony to what *Piper* and I had experienced. The dock is still slippery, and I take particular precautions to remain fully balanced as I pull the boat out of the water and hoist it onto my shoulders. On my way up the ramp with the boat on my shoulder, I focus as always on the white alder tree. It, too, is covered with frost, making a pretty welcome. It is Sunday, and it's winter; there has been no one else at the boathouse. I clean up, pack up, and drive home past Three Fingers and Whitehorse Mountains, now in bright sunshine.

Icicles along the Rail

⅄ ⅄ ⅄

I didn't row yesterday. That was Saturday, usually a good day to go; I can row longer, and there are often others out on the water. But it was windy and raining. I went to the boathouse thinking that I might get inspired to go anyway, but I just couldn't overcome the negative inertia, and I turned around and went home. As the day went on, improving weather provided a growing enticement to get on the water. Today there is a big storm in the forecast, increasing rain showers with winds up to seventy miles per hour during the day, and the TV newscasters are warning us to stay inside and be sure to have plenty of flashlight batteries. However, motivated by the embarrassment of my decision yesterday, I really want to go. If I can get on the water early enough, maybe I can get a row in before things get too bad.

The sky is cloudy as I drive to the boathouse, but those clouds rise as they travel east, revealing the mountains below, appearing in stark black and white. The flags on the several poles along the river give a mixed message about the wind, but there is nothing to overcome my commitment. As I ready *Piper* for the row, I can hear the singing of the frogs in a nearby pond recently awakened from their winter hibernation. I carry the boat down to the water, put her in, and shove off. The weather isn't so bad right now.

Boathouse from an Early-Morning Launch

I hit the water just before high tide, and there is still a bit of an upstream current helping me along. As is my usual choice, I turn down Steamboat Slough. The slough can be a good place to minimize the effect of wind. There are places where the breeze is noticeable, but there are others where the particular angle of the river in relation to the direction of the wind allows the trees along the bank to provide protection. As compensation for my cowardice of yesterday, I decide to row farther than usual, past Turnaround Tree, past the old barn on the west side of the river, down to the I-5 bridge and back.

In late winter, the dead grasses and reeds detach from the living plants, making room for new growth. Lifted off by the high tides, they wash into the river, where they gather together in bundles. Because the tide is very high right now, there are lots of these bundles on the river. I try to avoid them, but every now and again I pass through a patch; one encounter leaves a long reed caught around my skeg; another encounter wraps one over an oar. Lurking among the reed and grass bundles are some smaller logs, hard to see because they are sitting so low in the water. At the last second, I see one. I dig the oars into the water, bringing the boat to a stop but not fast enough. *Bang*, the bow of the boat hits the log; not too big, the log slips easily under the boat. *Bang* again, it hits the skeg and then slides away.

As I near the end of the row, just as I pass under the I-5 bridge, I see what looks like my own wake growing larger and now moving up toward me. Reaching just about to my stern, the wave parts, and a large harbor seal rolls out of the water, gives me a quick look, and rolls back into the water A few moments later, it surfaces again and swims casually away. I have had close encounters like this on a number of occasions; more often, it is just a simple glance as I row by. Harbor seals are a constant companion on the river at all times of the year. Even when they don't come in close to me, I sense that they are always aware of my presence. I think they are sensing the movement of the water I cause with my wake and have come by to explore, hoping that I am a big fish.

Rowing to the dock, I notice that the clouds have gotten lower. There is still not a lot of wind, but it is good that I am finishing up now. I land, lift the boat onto my shoulders, and head up the ramp. As I do, it begins to rain—perfect timing. By the time I get home, the wind has come up, and I resolve to heed the warning of the TV newscasters and stay inside for the rest of the day, listening to the wind howl. I was lucky that my power stayed on.

I use a Speed Coach to help me with my rowing. With a tiny propeller glued to the bottom of the boat and some amazing electronics, the Speed Coach measures and records the stroke rate, the time and distance of an outing, and the speed through the water. It has helped me improve and maintain my rowing technique. I will often look down and find that I am going slower than I had hoped and question, *Am I keeping my back straight? Am I not stretching my arms far enough aft before the catch where I dig the oars into the water and begin the pull? Is my stroke not the most efficient coordination of my legs, back, and arms, or do I just need to work harder?*

For me, the Speed Coach is also important for measuring the distance of my rows. In rowing on the river, it is not enough to know how far it is along the river to my turnaround spot. The current makes it a much longer row heading upstream and a much shorter row heading downstream. Along with helping me with my technique, the Speed Coach tells me how far I row through the water.

For the last six years, I have been keeping track of the distance through the water of each of my rows and adding this together as motivation to keep at it. I found that in the course of a year, I could row a thousand miles or more. Knowing that I need to chip away at the thousand miles helps to get me up in the dark and cold of a winter morning and get out there.

A couple of years ago, I also started using a runner's GPS watch to track my speed and distance along the land for comparison with the data from my Speed Coach, which measures my speed and distance through the water. Using the two instruments together gives me a good measure of how the currents are affecting my progress. When working against the current, my speed along the land can slow to five, four, or maybe even down to three-plus miles per hour, while my speed through the water remains relatively constant, somewhere between six and seven-plus miles per hour, depending on which boat I am rowing and my energy level at the time. With the current, while rowing at the same speed through the water, my speed along the land can reach eight, nine, and very occasionally ten miles per hour.

There is a lot of variation in the currents on the Snohomish River. The basic flow of the river depends on how much water flows out of the Cascade Mountains into the Skykomish and Snoqualmie Rivers, which join to form the Snohomish River and what is added by the Pilchuck River, which joins the Snohomish a little further downstream. Melting snow can provide a good current, particularly in the spring. A good rain anytime can make the water run fast, brown with soil from upstream. The river current is also affected by the ebb and flood of the tide. An ebb tide will significantly increase the river's flow. A flood tide, particularly after a deep low tide and with greater effect in the summer, when it rains less often and the snow melt is minimal, can produce a substantial upriver current. In seasons when the basic flow is strong, the river might not flow upriver even in a strong flood, but a rower can often find relief from the full force of the downstream current by choosing to row during the flood.

⅄⅄⅄

It can be hard to find a day to go rowing in winter. Cold weather, except in the extremes, cand be accommodated with more layers of clothing, but the rare appearance of ice in the river, and the more common strong winds and heavy rains can make it difficult to schedule a time to go out or add to the difficulty when I do. However, on those days that really aren't so pleasant, I can usually congratulate myself for just getting out there, and every winter does have those occasional days that are truly rewarding.

2

Spring

I AM NOT WAITING for the equinox; it's spring. My brother in Massachusetts may still be shoveling snow, but here in the Northwest, it has been getting warmer, and things are changing. You can see the buds on the trees, but the best sign of spring is more rowers on the water. There are more women and men getting involved in the masters rowing groups, and the Everett Rowing Association's junior rowing teams, girls and boys from the high schools, are beginning practice for this year's competitions. However, the final guarantee that it is spring will be found on the river.

Once *Piper* is ready to launch, I take a trip to the dock with my oars and water bottle. Upon arrival, I see one of those signs of spring, a pair of mallards standing there. They won't be in my way, so I invite them to stay, but their better sense tells them to keep their distance from humans, and they give me a quack and fly off a short distance. I go back to the boathouse, lift *Piper* to my shoulders, carry her down to the dock, and launch.

I notice that the current is quite strong. There are only intermittent clouds in the sky now, but there has been a lot of rain in the last few days, and the warmer temperatures in the mountains have added lots of melted snow to the river flow. That is going to really slow my progress upstream. But these heavy currents are going to affect my travel in other ways as well. The large amount of water rushing through the river channel causes eddies that swirl this way and that as it flows. I can see the trail left by my boat wash back and forth as I row. Often, I feel the whole boat jerk to one side and then the other as I row through the stronger eddies. Unlike other kinds of boats, the center of buoyancy of a shell, the point around which it rocks back and forth in the waves, is below the center of gravity, center of all the weight, somewhere a little above my waist I'm thinking. That means that that swerving back and forth can lead, as it has on more than one occasion, to capsizing. I keep my body loose and shift my weight to be sure that the center of gravity stays above the center of balance. I also keep a tight hand on the oars and take short strokes to be sure I can grab a hold of the water on one side if I start to fall over toward the other side.

There is less current in Steamboat Slough than there is in the main river, and the ride gets much smoother as I make the turn and head down. I can't help but notice the activity of the birds. They know it's spring. I see three mergansers swimming along by the river bank, one female with two male companions. Further on I see two eagles perched on the limb of a high tree. For a while I have only been seeing them by themselves; something is definitely going on now. Here comes a pair of Canada geese flying toward me from downriver, honking as they pass overhead.

Two Eagles on Piling

It has been light for some time, but the sun has just begun to rise over the mountains to the east. Still behind the trees as I row along the river, it becomes fully exposed in between gray, orange, and yellow clouds as I pass an opening between the trees. I make it to Turnaround Tree, turn around, and head home The sun is now above the trees, now shining on the still-bare limbs of the red and white alder trees and the occasional birch trees that grow on the west bank of the slough. Leaf buds have just begun to appear.

There are many species of birds around this time of year, and on this row, I am enjoying watching them fly overhead. There are always seagulls around, gliding whenever possible, with a very controlled stroking of their wings as needed to stay aloft. There are also lots of ducks. In contrast to the seagulls, ducks have to work harder to stay aloft, frantically flapping their wings as they speed across the river behind me. Particularly noticeable are the mergansers; unlike other ducks, they always fly low along the water. Of the birds I see on the river, the heron is the most unique in its flight. Its long neck, a valuable tool for catching fish, must be a problem in the air, but the heron makes it work by folding that neck in a tight S shape, becoming as graceful in flight as any bird. It is not always possible to tell which kind of a bird I am looking at. Right now I am looking at two large birds fly across the river behind me and land in a tree together. I can't tell what they are; all I could see was their dark shapes against the sky as they flew. I can tell by their shape that they aren't eagles; I think they are hawks of some kind, maybe a pair of ospreys.

Reaching the main river, I turn for home and find the current still strong and having its effects on the path of my boat. I almost row into a lone Canada goose. It squawks and flies a short distance, lands, and swims around idly, clearly irritated by my interruption. I am guessing that it is standing by a partner who is sitting on a nest somewhere nearby. Over there I see two eagles, each sitting on an old piling along the side of the river. One calls out and then flies over to join the other. They sit there chest to chest, each looking out in a different direction as if the other didn't exist.

Behind me on the river are the junior boys crews, two eights and a quad. I start pulling harder to test myself but am quickly passed. It is inspiring to see the coordinated strength of these boys producing such power as the boats speed by. I am sure those eagles were enjoying the show as well. The prize for being first back to the dock is to be able to pull out first. I have to wait a bit, but the boys work very quickly, and it doesn't take long before I have *Piper* up on her racks, and I am done for the day.

⅄⅄⅄

It is a Friday, and daylight savings time has arrived since my last row, robbing me of an hour of sleep and making sunrise later by the clock. The forecast is ideal, and looking out my window at the new 5:00 a.m., I see the sky full of stars. The weather is too perfect not to go for a row before heading for that office chair. As I drive to the boathouse, the dark shapes of the mountains against the very first light give me a preview of the row to come. It is still quite dark when I get to the boathouse, and the Morning Glories rowing group, locked into its hour on clock time, has again lost their daylight and is back on their rowing machines. I ready *Piper* in the very early light and head down the ramp. A clear sky overnight has allowed the earth's heat to radiate away, and there is frost on the dock, and caution is required.

The launch goes smoothly, and I head upriver. The sky is clear but for a few thin clouds; the rising sun gives them a rose-colored tint, which is mirrored in the calm water. As the sun rises, brightening up the sky, the color of the clouds turns to orange. As I make the turn into the slough, I see Mount Olympus and the rest of the Olympic range bathed orange in the sun. As the slough bends this way and that, there is just a short distance where Mount Rainier again appears, only to be lost as I round the next turn.

Reflections on a Calm River

Mount Rainier from Steamboat Slough

I see something leave the west bank and start swimming across the water. I had seen that same thing in about the same place last week; this must be near its home. It is not a bird, and it's not behaving like a seal. I slow down, hoping to find out what it is. Suddenly it rises out of the water and slaps its tail and dives out of sight; it's a beaver. Rowing on, I pass Eagle Tree and see just one eagle, whereas for a couple of trips I had been seeing two. I bet this guy is standing watch for a partner sitting in a nest somewhere nearby.

I row to Turnaround Tree and head home. The tide is pretty low, and I can see exposed along the bank the gnarled roots of the trees that line the slough. Passing some shallows, I also see the new green river grasses beginning to grow. Above, I can see that those buds I have been seeing on the trees have begun to blossom into leaves. My passing disturbs a pair of mergansers. The trios and quartets I have been seeing on earlier rows seem now to have divided themselves into matched pairs. Instead of flying way off down the river, this pair just flies a short distance. I bet there is a nest not far off. A little further along, I encounter a pair of Canada geese; they, too, don't go far and must also have a nest that needs protecting.

Tree Roots Exposed at Low Tide

Rowing for home in the main river, I have Mount Rainier in view behind me just off to the west now in bright sunlight with Mount Baker in my forward-view mirror in the front. It is still calm, and the river reflects the bright blue sky. There is still frost on the float when I land. I see the footprints I left during my launch. But I also see that I haven't been the only one using the float in the predawn. There are the unmistakable three large toes of a heron. Walking up the ramp, I see that the large white alder tree at the head of the ramp is beginning to show its new leaves. Today was a true visual highlight.

⅄ ⅄ ⅄

"Clear with just a chance of morning fog in the a.m." is the forecast. For where I row, that chance is usually pretty high. For the Morning Glories, that usually means another day on the rowing machines because it would be impossible for their coach to keep everyone in view. I am going out if I can see the trees on the other side of the river, and I will keep going as long as I can see both sides of the river. That is a pretty high tolerance and although I have sometimes decided from home not to go because of the fog, I don't think I have ever turned back once I started.

My test is passed, and I am off. I always know where I am, but with the limited visibility, I find myself straying over to one side of the river. I correct my course but before long find myself having strayed over to the other side. I am going to experience that several times again throughout the row. My forward-view mirror is fogging up, and it is not long before I have to stop and wipe it clear with the handkerchief I have folded up in my sock for just that purpose. I will be repeating that several times during this row.

At first light I could see fairly well through the fog, but now the sun is higher, and its reflection on the fog droplets has made the fog seem denser, and the visibility is worse. I can still see both sides of the river, and I still know where I am, but I do need to wipe off the mirror again to be sure that there isn't a log with my name on it or, worse, other rowers heading my way. It is still calm, and the trees along the bank are reflected in the water against the backdrop of the fog. It is too foggy to see the sun, but in the neighborhood where it should be, its rays illuminate the fog with a faint rosy glow.

Trees Appearing on a Calm, Foggy Morning

It was quite cool when I started, but it has warmed a bit, and I have generated some heat with my exercise. I am feeling a little overheated, and I need to remove a layer of clothing, not an easy job. The change of attire is going to take two hands, those same two hands I use to hold on to the oars to keep the boat from tipping over. To accomplish this feat, I press my chest up against the two oars, hoping that will keep them steady while I take off my windbreaker, remove the down vest, and then replace the windbreaker. With my two arms behind my back, one hand pulling the windbreaker sleeve off of the other arm, I feel particularly vulnerable. If one of those oars gets loose, I'll end up swimming. Success—this time at least. Whew!

Whak, whak, whak. The fog has brought me up unexpectedly on twelve Canada geese that were casually swimming in the river. Clearly irritated by the interruption, they nevertheless move over and let me through. With visibility restricted, there isn't much other wildlife to be seen on this trip. I concentrate on my rowing and where I am going, and I am soon back to the dock. I land and carry *Piper* up to the boathouse. The Midmorning masters rowing group has their boats ready to launch but is waiting for the fog to lift just a bit more. While I clean up and put *Piper* onto her rack, the fog lifts some more, and as I head to my car, I see the Midmorning rowers heading out.

The one thing I did see when I was rowing was that the skunk cabbages with their big leaves and bright yellow blossoms have begun to appear. This is the sign for me to take *Piper* to the garage for use in some open-water expeditions and replace her at the boathouse with *Molly*. *Piper* is more stable and easier to manage than the longer and slimmer *Molly* and has a bailing device that draws out any water that might splash into the cockpit. It is also easier to right and reboard in the event of a capsize. For safety's sake, it was good to have *Piper* along on my late-fall, winter, and early-spring rows, but it is *Molly's* turn. *Molly* is a flat-water shell built by Pocock Racing Shells. She is named *Molly*, the name I had proposed for the girl child we never had.

Molly

⅄ ⅄ ⅄

There is snow forecast for the east coast, but the TV meteorologist here has been promising a few nice days with temperatures into the seventies, and I hope to get out a couple of times this week. The morning twilight is early enough so that I can get on the water at about 6:00 a.m. As I carry my boat to the water, I see the Morning Glories readying their boats to get on the water as well. This is my first time out on *Molly* this year. She is definitely faster than *Piper*, but the extra length and slimmer hull that makes for that extra speed make the boat more tender, and it is taking me a while to get used to it again.

It is still a little chilly as I start out in the predawn twilight, but it is not long before my exercise makes me comfortable. The water is calm, and the sky is hazy but clear, a beautiful morning to be on the water. The leaves on the trees are more prominent; the lighter green of new leaves stands out in contrast to the branches of their neighboring evergreens. The shrubs and vines along the banks that were brown all winter long have also turned green with new growth. There is also a number of flowering trees along the river now in full bloom.

I see another creature working along the edge of the river and pause to watch. When it sees me, it slaps its tail and dives out of sight. I am guessing that it is the same beaver I saw the other day. A little further, I see two other creatures swimming along, one next to the bank to my left and the other pretty far away on the other side of the river. They are not acting like seals; they could be otters, but it is most likely that they are some other beavers. They both slip quietly out of sight, leaving me guessing.

I started out at just about high tide, and there was almost no current as I began my row. A little ways out, I cross a wave line across the river, the beginnings of the downstream current. Down the slough, I can see a two-inch wet line on the trees along the bank, confirming the change. There will most certainly be a good current helping me along when I get back to the main river. While I was out, the Morning Glories launched and went for their row. As I reach the main river, I see them on the water, three quads, two rowed by women and one by men, and a couple of singles. It is a pleasure to see other rowers on the river.

There are a series of tall light poles along the west side of the main river. There has always been a lot of bird activity on these poles, and recently I had seen a new collection of branches at the top of one of them. As I row by today, I can see its purpose. There is the white head of an eagle appearing above the branches of this nest. On the next pole over sits another eagle keeping watch. As the seasons progress, it is going to be fun to see the family develop.

Eagle in Her Nest on a Light Pole

A couple of years ago on another light pole further upriver, I got to watch a couple of ospreys raise their young. Like the eagles today, one of the couple sat on the nest while the mate watched from nearby. During the summer, I could see the two offspring in the nest and watch them grow. By fall, they were gone. Last year, there seemed to be a dispute between the ospreys and the eagles. I saw a number of eagles, but my only memory of an osprey that year was seeing one fly across the river with a large stick in its beak for a nest somewhere away from this part of the river. I can still see the uninhabited remains of the osprey nest. It looks like this year it's eagle territory.

It's not far from the eagle's nest to the dock. As I land, I see two seals playing together in the middle of the river. A few moments later, as I get ready to lift *Molly* out of the water, I see a big swirl in the water a short way off. The two seals surface, give me a quick glance, and swim away. As I walk up the ramp, I see two Canada geese sitting on one of the breakwater logs, talking to each other. At the top of the ramp, I glance as always at the big white alder tree across the road, its leaves now in full bloom. I clean up and head to work.

Welcoming Alder in Spring

⅄⅄⅄

It is another one of those days when the forecast isn't too friendly: showers with increasing wind. However, I have been having pretty good luck these days staying out from under the showers. The wind doesn't look too deadly, and I might be able to avoid it if I get on the water early. Driving to the boathouse, I see some pretty dark clouds, but it isn't raining, and the breeze right now looks manageable. It's not like I am going to be out in open water; being down on the water below the river banks, and the trees along it, protects me from the full force of the wind, and the curving path of the river prevents any large buildup of waves.

I launch and head up the river. I haven't gone too far when I see a large black cloud moving from west to east behind me. It is quite a distance off, and it looks pretty well self-contained. I think it is going to be best for me to keep upriver of it. It is moving pretty fast and will probably be gone by the time I return to the dock. Oh, I see a couple of lightning strikes come from the cloud; I am definitely going to stay upriver.

Watch Out—There Is a Storm Coming

The wind is against me on the river, but it is heading in the same direction as the current, so the waves it is generating aren't getting too large. It is necessary to lift the oars a little further out of the water on the recovery to get them above the waves. That doesn't always succeed; every now and again the oar hits a wave, tilting the boat just slightly to the other side. It's still manageable, but it does make me recall why I enjoy rowing on calm water. Waves don't usually get as large on Steamboat Slough, so I turn and take my usual route.

It's becoming clear that I didn't beat the wind; it has been getting stronger and stronger. With the many turns of the slough, the waves are not getting too big, but it is definitely having its effect on my boat speed. As I'm heading down the slough, the wind is now behind me, adding measurably to my speed. The greater density of the wavelets caused by an increase in the wind makes the water darker under a gust; I can see these *cat's paws* move toward me across the water and feel the added pressure of the wind on my body and its effect on the boat when it hits. I am happy to see that the black cloud has moved on. The sky now is covered with the dramatic hills and valleys on the underside of the clouds in their varying shades of grays.

Down a ways, Steamboat Slough does straighten out in a direction parallel with the wind, allowing some significant waves to build. It might have been best to turn around early, but I challenge myself and row all the way to Turnaround Tree, now feeling the slap of the oars on the waves and the consequent rolling of the boat back and forth. Arriving at my objective, I turn and head back. Until I get to the main river, the wind and waves will be against me. I give up my thoughts of a smooth and fast row and settle down to what is just the work ahead for me.

I finally make it to the main river. I can see that the waves have gotten larger than they were when I rowed up. I pause for a minute or two to catch my breath and ready myself for the final dash home. Now I am off. The wind is behind me, and the boat is now sort of surfing down the waves. I say "sort of" because the waves aren't pushing me straight ahead but rather first off to one side and then off to the other. It's best to take short strokes and keep the oars high on the recovery. I pass a man walking the river trail. I hear him yell, "Are you crazy?" I wish I had that excuse. I feel somewhat secure in the knowledge that both the wind and current are in my favor and that even if I just sat there, not rowing at all, focused solely on keeping my balance, I would still eventually get back to the dock. It is also just a short swim to the nearest shore. However, I am able to keep up a steady stroke rate, and these waves are still nothing compared to what they would be in open water.

A large flock of birds high in the sky, probably Canada geese, is being affected by the wind as well. A gust of wind hits them, distorting their formation. The birds stay in their lines, but the lines are now bent up and down and off to the left and right. As the birds work to get back into formation, another gust arrives, creating additional distortions. The formation now has the look of abstract art. When the gust passes, the geese, without leaving their lines, adjust their flight to move back into their V formation.

I need to get back. I reach the dock and pull *Molly* out of the water. As I'm heading up the ramp, the wind pushes on the boat, and I struggle to keep it straight. I manage to get it onto the slings, dried off, and onto its rack in the boathouse. This has been one of those rows that I am feeling better about now that it's done. Well, it didn't rain.

⅄ ⅄ ⅄

It's going to be one of those special spring days: clear, calm, and northwest warm once the sun gets up. A day like this can bring extra joy to a row. The morning twilight makes its appearance early this time of year, and I have set an early alarm to try to beat the sun to the boathouse. I will arrive at 5:15 a.m. and will be able to get on the water a full two hours earlier than was possible in January. The Morning Glories row this morning, but they won't arrive for quite a while.

As I carry *Molly* down the ramp, I see two Canada geese pacing around in the now quite tall river grass; between them in constant motion are four babies, the first sign of new life I have seen this year. The sun isn't visible yet, but as I seat myself on the sliding seat and insert my feet into the foot stretchers, I see through the haze that it has risen far enough to illuminate Mount Baker in pink far to the north. I dig my outboard oar into the water to catch the current that will pull me away from the dock and out into the river.

Calm Start, Mount Baker in the Distance

It is completely calm, and the blue sky and the few light clouds are perfectly matched in the reflection on the river, distorted only by the splash of my oars and the light wake of the boat. I row over to the west side of the river to check on the eagles. I can see the white head of one eagle sticking out from the nest high on the light pole with the mate sitting guard on another pole nearby. Further on, as I row past the old osprey nest, I am surprised to see a bird fly in with a branch. I was wrong; the ospreys did come back. I guess the two species have reached an understanding; it will be nice to see how they coexist to raise their respective families.

Sun Rising over the River Fog

It is still calm when I turn down Steamboat Slough. The sun is fully up and following me from the other side of the trees along the riverbank. There are occasional patches of a light river fog, but the visibility is not affected. The vegetation along the banks is now fully green, and the wild roses are in bloom. It looks like there is snow on the river. The alder trees have released their cottony seed pods, and they are collected into small patches all over the river.

Alder Seeds Like Snow on the River

I hear a splash from up ahead and off to my right. It is no doubt one of the river critters irritated by my interruption. One of the disadvantages of rowing is only getting to look ahead in the occasional glance into the forward-view mirror. The seals never seem to mind my presence, but the beavers and otters see me coming and, most of the time, manage to disappear just about the time I learn that they are there.

I can see in my mirror that I am coming up on a pair of Canada geese idly swimming along. As I near, one of them calmly swims off to the side. The other, spooked by my approach, squawks loudly and flies off a short distance. However, the bird has landed directly in my path, and I am quickly upon it. As I approach, again it squawks, again it flies a short distance, and again it lands directly in my path. Another squawk, another takeoff, and another landing directly in my path. This drama repeats itself three or four times before the goose flies over to the side of the river out of my way, where it watches angrily as I row by.

I have rowed far enough; it is time to turn around and head back. The sun is now well above the trees, reflecting brilliantly in the calm water and making it a little difficult to see at times. I can see a heron up ahead sitting peacefully on an old piling on the side of the river. Unnerved by my approach, it flies off to a more secure location. Further along, I see four Canada geese near the riverbank swimming herd on a fleet of new babies.

As I turn down the river toward the dock, I meet the Morning Glories rowing group heading out. There are two quads, one men's and one women's, a man and woman in singles, and two women in a double. Their coach, shouting occasional instructions, keeps an eye on all from her launch, while her husky dogs watch the proceedings from the bow. It's good to see others enjoying this great physical experience on this beautiful river. There are others out enjoying the morning. Far off to the south, I see a colorful hot-air balloon rising high in the sky. Before long, I see a second.

I am soon back at the dock. As I hoist *Molly* overhead, a seal swims close by and gives me a curious eye. I walk up the ramp, greeted again by the alder tree at the head. *Molly* goes on her rack, and I head to the office.

3

Summer

SUMMER HAS OFFICIALLY come. However, in the Northwest, reliable warm weather doesn't always arrive for a while. Right now there is a low-pressure cell centered just off the coast, bringing cooler than normal temperatures and waves of rain up from the south. The forecast is for a short period of relief tomorrow morning before a heavy rain front comes in. I lay out my rowing gear, get to bed early, rise at four, and leave the house at five. The sky is clear, and the mountains are out, but it is a little cooler than it should be for this time of year, and there is a little breeze, so I need an extra layer to be comfortable.

As I carry *Molly* down the ramp, I encounter several families of Canada geese—mothers, fathers, and their now fast-growing offspring—feeding in the river grasses along the shore. They don't appear to be disturbed at all by my arrival. I launch and head upriver against a strong current. This is my first row after attending a three-day session at the Craftsbury Sculling Center in upstate Vermont, and I am anxious to try to adopt the things I learned. They had much to tell me, but I came away focused on gliding longer between strokes and keeping the oars closer to the surface during the stroke. The current is pretty strong, and the swirling eddies that I encounter push the boat back and forth; it is important that I keep my upper body synchronized with the swaying of the boat to keep it stable. The current will be much calmer once I turn into Steamboat Slough, one of the reasons I like to row there.

My first destination is the eagles' nest. I haven't seen any birds around the nest for a couple of weeks now; I am afraid that something interrupted this eagle pair's efforts to raise their family and they have moved on. Rowing on, I see that a large barge has been parked along the shore, right under the osprey nest. It appears there are plans to load it with dirt. The ospreys aren't obviously present as they had been; I am afraid that the activity around the barge has caused them to move on as well. The eagles and ospreys are gone, but one of the nice things about summer is the presence of people walking along a trail along the east side of the river, frequently with their dogs and sometimes with kids on bikes or in strollers.

As I make the turn into the slough, an eagle flies right overhead and then soars out over the river, its white head and tail brightly lit by the sun. A little further on, I see another eagle perched awkwardly on a high tree branch, two crows flying around it, obviously irritated at its presence. These are the first two eagles I have seen in some time. Perhaps they are the two that abandoned that nest.

One of the first things you come to on the slough is a line of boats moored on a dock along the south shore, some work boats and some pleasure craft. Some of these serve as homes for their owners; others have just been placed there, I gather, because moorage is cheap. For some of these boats, this is the end of the line. Over the years, I have seen boats parked here until they sink. Some of these derelicts have been removed by the state department of ecology, but a number of others are still where they went down,

Sunken Boats

monuments to their owners' disrespect for the value the boat had when it was useful and irresponsibility to that place in nature where they were left. Boats are just collections of wood, fiberglass, aluminum, and steel, but they are human creations and have been part of human activity since the very early days of our species. Boats of some sort have been part of my life from my early childhood. It is sad to see these thoughtlessly abandoned. I will feel a little relieved when I get beyond them.

As I row into the more natural surroundings, I start to think about my Craftsbury lessons: glide more between each stroke and keep my hands low when I pull to keep the oars from digging too deep in the water. Since rowing is normally such an unthinking process for me, I have to keep reminding myself to concentrate on my lessons. My Speed Coach confirms that I am going faster with less exertion when I do it right.

The cattails along the banks are growing tall now. Occasionally among them I see a slender red-leafed plant; it makes a nice contrast to all the green. I wish I knew what that plant was. The tweeting of the sparrows is almost constant, and just now I see two of them flying circles around each other. Over there in the dead branches of a tree is an osprey keeping watch. At another place on the river, I can hear but not see a woodpecker tapping away on a tree. Now again is that brief opportunity to see Mount Rainier, orange in the morning sun. This is going to be a good day to row around Otter Island.

Just before Ebey Slough joins Steamboat Slough, it branches into two streams, creating Otter Island. The Everett Rowing Association sponsors a row around the island every fall, followed by a big feast. Now on my own, I row up Ebey Slough for about a half of a mile to the entrance of the other stream. As I near the entrance to that other stream, my oar catches on the limb of a sunken tree I hadn't seen; the boat tips to the side. I grab for the water with my other oar and manage to avoid capsizing. Because the current is running strong, my timing has to be good to get safely into the narrow entrance to that other stream. This is definitely the smaller stream, and it gets pretty shallow.

A few years ago, I did this trip at near low tide and had to carry the boat for about a hundred feet over the muddy bottom. The tide isn't so low now, but I can see several deadheads sticking out of the water and one ripple in the water where another lurks just beneath the surface. My carefully chosen course gets me around all of these, and I make it back to the wider and deeper Steamboat Slough and head back to the dock. As I stop for a short rest, I can hear the soft coo of a morning dove.

I again focus on my Craftsbury lessons and am rowing smoothly. Behind me I see an eagle fly over the river and hover near the water, focused on a particular spot. It looks about to dive but changes its mind and flies up and lands in a tree. Rowing a little further, I hear a long, loud squawk. I never saw it, but I am guessing that it was a heron expressing its displeasure about something. I make it back to the main river and head for the dock. I can see Mount Rainier again, but this time, above it but off to the east a bit, there is a lenticular cloud, an isolated round cloud consisting of condensed water vapor in the air flowing up over the mountain. That forecast for the rain and clouds to swing around the low-pressure cell and hit us sometime today is probably correct. I head to the dock, put *Molly* away, and go home. The clouds did fill in, and although it never got windy like it does in winter or spring, it sure rained.

⅄⅄⅄

Summer can be a good time for some extended rows. It's a beautiful day with white clouds in a blue sky. I decide to row around Ebey Island again, about a 15.3-mile trip along the land. The perfect time to row around Ebey Island occurs when a fading up-river current boosts you along until you reach the entrance to the Ebey Slough and then changes to a downriver current to get you back home. A look at the tide tables tells me that that is not going to happen for some time. Indeed, today it looks like I will be facing an outgoing king tide where an extra-high tide flows out to an extra-low minus tide, creating an extra-strong downstream current. However, if I am going to do an extended row, this is still the best choice, and I will at least get the benefit of a helpful current down the Ebey Slough.

It is Saturday, and there are number of masters rowers at the boathouse. I get launched while they are organizing themselves and probably won't see them on the water; they will finish their row long before I am done. The swirling and fast-moving current holds my attention as I proceed up the main river, and I am constantly having to make small course corrections as I row. A comparison of the through-the-water distance on the Speed Coach and the along-the-land distance on the GPS tells me what kind of a current I am dealing with. I figure that my travel through the water is about a third further than my travel along the land.

I stay on the river, pass the turnoff to Steamboat Slough, and soon come to Everett's river waterfront. Once upon a time, it was busy here. It was the center for lots of boats carrying passengers and cargo up and down the river and onshore businesses dealing with the people and goods that arrived. These days, it appears that there is little commercial business this far up the river. There are boats, mostly used in the fishing industry, parked there permanently, unused docks, many abandoned buildings, and onshore piles of unknown materials. The area has a great potential for recreational uses, and Everett has plans in the works. Right now it's a little sad to see the area going to waste.

Passing under the Highway US 2 bridge, I soon come to an old derrick used by many rowers as a good place to turn around, but I am going on. On the east side of the river, there are farmlands. There are cows grazing along the river bank; one or two of them look over at me as I pass. Over on the west side, there are endless rows of old moss-covered pilings with grass and an occasional small tree growing out of the top, put there long ago for purposes no longer known. I pass under the high-voltage power lines, three and a third miles along the land from where I launched but four and a half through the water. On the top of the tower on the west, I see my first eagle of the trip.

I reach the community of Lowell; now a part of Everett, it was once an independent port on the Snohomish River. The only signs today of the logging and other commerce that thrived there along the water are more of those pilings along the shore. The river makes a right-angle turn at Lowell, and I turn from southbound to eastbound to continue upriver.

Lowell

In another mile along the land, I reach the entrance to Ebey Slough. There are several deadheads at the entrance and, once the turn is made, two piling right in the middle of the channel. Careful navigation done with aid of my forward-view mirror gets me through, and I am on my way down the slough. To this point, I have rowed five and a half miles along the land and eight miles through the water. Happily, the current is now with me. Over there is another eagle sitting on another high-voltage power-line tower. Seen before during early-spring rows but now hidden in the leaves, there is an eagles' nest that has been active for a number of years.

The Ebey Slough flows first through farmland. I can't see much from my vantage point on the water below the riverbanks, but the trees are mostly gone, and I can see the tops of a couple of barns as I row by. The upper part of the Ebey Slough winds back and forth, and I find that I have to pull hard with one oar or the other to stay in the channel. Every now and again I realize that I have returned to my old habits and am not

Farm along Ebey Slough

using the form I learned at Craftsbury. It is going to be important to remind myself to think about it every now and again until it becomes habitual. My passage along the land is going much faster with the current in my favor, and it's not long before trees close in along both banks of the river.

Highway US 2 passes over Ebey Slough on two low bridges. I slow down to carefully aim for a path between their cement pilings. As I begin to pass under the bridge, hundreds of swallows fly into the air, circling around and around in all directions. Looking up underneath the bridge, I see their mud nests, and I row along, hoping not to disturb the birds any more than I already have.

Not far along on the west side of the slough is another one of those riverside marinas with a number of old boats that have been there a long time and are not likely to go to sea again. Passing on, I row back into farmlands. From my vantage point on the water, I can't see much right on the other side of the levee, but on the hill beyond, I can see homes on the outskirts of the town of Lake Stevens. At about twelve miles of my trip along the land, I reach the junction of the Ebey and Steamboat Sloughs. The current has been with me since leaving the main river. Nevertheless, on the trip as a whole, I have spent more of my time working against the current, and I have still rowed through the water a couple of additional miles, and it's time for a rest. With the noise of my rowing silenced, I can hear the swallows chirping and the tapping of a woodpecker. It's nice to be able to just sit here and not move and enjoy the scenery.

Rowing where I do is a little like driving on a road through a pretty countryside. The difference, of course, is that the path I am on is water, which reflects the trees and plants along the sides of the river and the sky in its center. These reflections are really sharp on the calm waters of an early morning. As I take a stroke and start *Molly* moving again, I feel encouraged in my venture by the fluffy white clouds in the bright blue sky above reflected clearly in the water I am rowing on.

It's about three miles along the land back to the dock. The current is against me in Steamboat Slough, but once in the main river, it helps me finish swiftly. When I get back to the dock, my GPS tells me that I have traveled 15.77 miles along the land, and my Speed Coach shows that I rowed 17.62 miles through the water. I'm going home and take it really easy for the rest of the day.

⅄⅄⅄

It is another beautiful morning, a little light north breeze, but it's warm, and the sky is clear. This is a good day to row around Smith and Spencer Islands. I start a little later than usual, but there are a number of groups going out, and I want to stay out of their way. The sun has long been up, but I can see a faint full moon just setting in the west. My trip starts downriver. It's a little after high tide, and I have a pretty strong current helping me along. I soon see the Morning Glories rowing group in two quads rowing upstream, and I head over to the side to let them pass.

As it is upriver, there are many pilings with no current purpose, but unlike upstream, there are a number of active businesses along the shore. This part of Everett retains its historic focus on muscle, big machines doing heavy work, leaving all that tech work for Seattle and points south. On the west side of the river is a large railroad yard where railcars carrying oil, coal, or cargo containers are being assembled and where the occasional passenger train speeds through. The first thing I come to on the east side is a large marina. Boats there are kept on land and place in the water at the request of their owners. There are a number of boats sitting at the dock, waiting for their owners to take them out on this beautiful day. Passing on, I come to a large barge being fed woodchips for a pulp mill and then a yard where logs are collected for transport to a saw mill.

In close succession, I pass under the highway bridge for State Route 529 and the railroad bridge that parallels it. Both are old through-truss bridges supported by networks of iron girders; the highway bridge draws open, and the railroad bridge pivots around for large boat traffic, not a problem for me. Once through there, the river widens out as it arrives at Port Gardner Bay, and I start looking for my course to the east. It gets very shallow here, and it is a good thing I'm here near high tide; I have run aground here on other trips.

Turning the point, I enter a large bay with pilings everywhere, some in rows a regular distance apart and others side by side as a breakwater. The human purpose long since over, they now provide perching and nesting for water fowl. I see occupied osprey nests on two of the pilings, others providing seagulls and other birds with a place to rest. There are also quite a few cormorants standing on the pilings, many with their wings outstretched, drying in the sun, an image apparently used by John Milton in *Paradise Lost* to represent Satan. Cruising through the water are lots of seals; over there is a mother with her young pup. Far behind me through the summer haze, I can see the Olympic Mountains with their snow all but gone.

I am never completely sure where to head until I see the derrick and dry dock of the boatyard on the west side of the entrance to the Steamboat Slough. The course adjusted, and a hundred more strokes bring me to another railroad bridge passing low over the river. I don't have to actually duck to get through, but the often-painted and now rusty span is right in my face as I clear. Three hundred feet further, I pass under the separate spans for the east and west travel on Highway SR 529 and in a couple of hundred yards more, under the high bridge for Interstate 5.

Now I am back in the more natural surroundings of Steamboat Slough with several miles of strong currents to fight. It is a long way, but all the navigational challenges have been met, and I let my mind drift off with only occasional interruptions to check on my rowing form. There is not much to see right here, a barn and farmhouse on the west side and a swampy area on the east—time to just row. It's about two miles to Turnaround Tree, my usual turnaround spot when coming the other way, and another half mile to Eagle Tree, where I would turn around years ago. I am feeling strong and relaxed.

Up ahead, I see a number of junior rowers from the Everett Rowing Association resting and listening to instructions from their coach from his outboard launch. There are a couple of doubles and a number of single sculls. I get by and a couple hundred yards past when they start coming in my direction. I start to row faster, but it soon becomes clear that these juniors are going to catch and pass me with ease. I console myself by remembering that I have rowed eight miles by this point, but on consideration I conclude it's the youth, energy, and training that take them past me and away. What a good time for a drink of water and a short rest.

From here, it's just looking like work. I am pretty tired, and it's getting hot. I find some inspiration by focusing on the form of my stroke. Looking around, it's also encouraging to see a heron standing patiently on a piling on the side of the river and a little later to have another give me a loud squawk as it flies across the river behind me. A little further along, I see a flock of Canada geese flying high overhead; I am imagining that a lot of these are this year's newborns being conditioned by their parents for their flight south this winter.

With my energies renewed, I finish the last mile against the current in Steamboat Slough and then turn down-current in the main river to finish my row to the dock. Those juniors I encountered earlier have their boats put away by the time I get my boat up from the water and are receiving an encouraging talk from their coach as I clean up and put *Molly* on her racks. It's time now to go home and get out of the heat.

⅄ ⅄ ⅄

The days of summer are marching along, and I have been wanting to take the extra time to row around Jetty Island. Jetty Island is a long, thin, sandy island at the end of the Snohomish River that runs between two and three thousand feet off the shore along much of the Port of Everett. It's a city park, and people go there to enjoy the sandy beaches and observe the birds that make it their home.

Arriving at the boathouse, I notice that the tide is quite low and, in talking to one of the other rowers, am reminded how shallow it is, particularly around the east end of Jetty Island. However, the tide is coming in, and it is going to take me a while to get down there. I am going to go down there and see what I find. I put *Molly* into the water and head out, passing around some of the Morning Glory rowers that launched just ahead of me.

Not far along, I pass close to an osprey perched in its nest on some pilings with its partner on another piling not far away. As I continue, I notice a number of other ospreys at work and a number of cormorants standing on pilings with their wings outstretched to dry. The sun is well up to the east with the mountains appearing below it as dark shapes against the blue sky. There is activity at the businesses along the river, but I am paying more attention to the state of the tides and worrying that I may be rowing into trouble.

Osprey on Nest, Partner Standing By

The river empties into the bay at the east end of Jetty Island, and I decide to try going around that end first and row around the island counterclockwise to learn early whether this expedition is going to work at all. The water is shallow, and I can see the bottom, but so far I am still floating. I can feel myself going slower in the shallows. The wave made by a boat moving through the water is more than a ripple above the surface; it's also a movement of water down under the boat. When that part of the wave comes against the bottom, it forces the energy back up, and the boat slows down. This is something a rower can really feel because it becomes harder to pull the oars through the water.

Uh-oh, the skeg has started dragging through the sand, but maybe it's only for a short distance...no, I am stuck. I can't make it through and have to turn back. The boat is still floating, barely; it's the skeg that is stuck. I take off my footwear, climb out, turn the boat around, and wade back the way I came for a hundred yards or so, pulling *Molly* behind. I think it's deep enough now, and I climb back in and start rowing again.

There is deeper water along the south side of Jetty Island, and I decide to at least row down to the west end. Jetty Island began as a breakwater of rocks built in the late 1800s to provide some protection to Everett Harbor. Material dredged out of the Snohomish River has been placed there, and over the years the river itself has contributed silt it washed down from the mountains. The original wall of rocks is pretty much covered with sand populated in places with shrubs and the occasional tree. A sandy beach surrounds the island, which is particularly evident during this low tide. Across on the mainland, I row past some industries; a shallow expanse with rows of pilings where logs are stored, far less now than in the past; a boat launch; a large marina for fishing boats and pleasure craft; some waterfront restaurants; and the Everett Naval Station. The trip along this side of the island is being slowed by the incoming tidal current, but I have made it to the end and have to decide what to do now.

If I try to continue around, I could run aground again. However, it's calm, and waters of the whole bay reflect the light blue of the sky; it will be nice to row out there even if I have to retreat and travel back the way I came. Besides, the tide is coming in and may increase the depth enough over the sandbar by the time I get there. I am going to do it.

As I start out, a seagull sees me while flying by, sets his course for mine, comes right up behind, and when right overhead, veers off in a new direction. Meanwhile, on the sandy beach of the island sits a large flock of its fellow seagulls, squawking loudly to one another. Even a hundred feet from shore, although deep enough for me, it's still pretty shallow. I see an object sticking out of the water ahead covered with barnacles; as I pass near, I realize I am passing over the remains of a wrecked ship and have to change course to avoid the chance of running into part of the structure hiding just below the surface of the water. Out in the bay, I stop to watch a large swarm of small seabirds flying around and around, this way and that, in no set pattern but always in perfect coordination.

Jetty Island is a popular launch site for kite surfers, and I recall dining at one of those waterfront restaurants and enjoying seeing glimpses of the kites flying through the sky with the surfer speeding across the waters of the bay below. Fortunately for me in my much slower trip, it is still almost completely calm. The rowing is easier without the waves, and the blue reflection of the sky provides a peaceful setting for my efforts.

I am nearing the area where I had to turn around, and it is encouraging to see that the sandbar that extended out into the bay here on the east end of the island isn't as prominent as it was. I can see the sandy bottom not far below, and the boat is slowing down from the shallows, but I only need to get a little further to be where it was deep enough before. My starboard oar hits the sand but still manages to pull through. Just a couple more strokes—one, two, three…whew, I made it to where I know it's deep enough.

The rest of the trip will be easier. It's not too far, and I am aided by the upstream current of the still-flooding tide. I pass two shells from the midmorning rowing group heading out. It is not long before I land at the dock, put *Molly* away, and head home.

4

Fall

THE CALENDAR TELLS me it's fall. But there have been other signs as well. We just had our first big fall rain, and our time with the sun is getting shorter at a rate of more than three minutes a day. Because my time is flexible, I can start my row a little later, now after the start of the Morning Glories' session. We are going to hit the water at about the same time because the darkness has kept them on rowing machines for the first part of their session. The sky was clear when I left the house, but as I approach the clubhouse, I encounter a third sign that it is fall: return of fog on the river. It's a light fog but a clear sign of what's to come. Once the Morning Glory rowers have shoved off, I take *Molly* down to the dock and shove off too.

River Reflections on a Calm Morning

Over to my left—remember I am facing backward—is a railroad engine being hooked up to its hundreds of freight cars. They are almost always there, and I have come not to give them much thought until, as now, I hear the *bang, bang, bang, bang* as each car is jerked into motion. The railroad runs right along the river for a ways. I am moving faster than the train as it starts, but I can see it picking up speed and gaining on me as it heads off where the tracks and river separate.

I am just going to do my usual row up the river, down Steamboat Slough, to Turnaround Tree, and return. It is a little cooler these days, so I am glad I am wearing my windbreaker. It occurs to me that this is just the first step to late-fall and winter rowing, when it will be much colder and I will be wearing more layers of heavier clothes. I am also thinking that I will have to challenge myself to get up in total darkness and hit the water at very first light. I tell myself not to be too negative; there will be some very nice rows here in the fall, and I will meet the challenges of winter when they come.

The river is in the last stages of a flooding tide, and I get a little assistance rowing up the river. The numbers on the Speed Coach are not what I would like; I am going a third of a mile slower than I have been. Well, I have been on holiday, away from the river for three weeks and eating too freely. The extra weight sinks the boat deeper into the water, and the loss of muscle tone is making it harder than usual to move the extra water aside.

As I row down Steamboat Slough, I can see that the leaves on the red alder trees are beginning to turn. Northwest foliage in the fall is nothing like the beautiful fall foliage in the New England. The native trees of this area just turn at best to a sad kind of yellow and then brown, or they just shrivel and fall. That's too bad, but I console myself with the thought that I will find days in winter to get out on the water when my northeastern counterparts are finding only ice on the water. The Northwest trees in the fall may be disappointing, but I can see reds, yellows, oranges, and purples against the fading green in the bushes along the bank. I can also pick out the wild roses, now with their plump, reddish-orange seed pods. The cattails, too, are quite striking with their fully mature brown seed heads standing high over the now-wilting leaves. The ubiquitous green of summer has been replaced for just a while with a diversity of color.

My attention turns inward, and interspersed with thoughts about the troubles of the world, I concentrate on trying to get my speed back: stretching further back on the recovery for a longer hold on the water during the stroke, keeping the oars shallow, timing the hardest exertion for the point where the oars have the greatest leverage, and remembering to let the boat glide to get the full effect of that exertion. These things do seem to bring back some of the speed I had lost. I make it to Turnaround Tree, turn around, and head back.

It's mostly just work from here, but in time, I am back. The Morning Glories had finished their row and have left the boathouse, but the mid-morning group is bringing their oars down to the dock as I arrive. I put *Molly* away and head off to the office. I am finishing a lot later than I was in late spring and summer, and I don't have time to go home to clean up. Starting today, I will be showering at work.

⅄⅄⅄

In contrast to my last time out, today looks like a perfect day for a row. Invasions by a low-pressure front with its clouds and showers are becoming more and more common, but we often get a nice day or sometimes just a part of a nice day in between. When I arrive at the boathouse, the sun is out, and it's calm. The tide is way out, and it is a long way down the ramp to the dock. Hopefully, the tide will have come in some by the time I return so that I won't have too steep a climb up the ramp. I launch *Molly* and head upriver. There is still just a bit of downstream current to contend with.

The low tide has exposed a sandy beach along the west side of the river. There are two separate groups of Canada geese encamped there, no doubt making preparations for their winter trip south. It's good to see these geese again before they leave. It's Sunday, and I am probably going to be the only rower on the river, but across the river from the geese, there are a number of people walking on the trail, enjoying the nice weather.

Turning down Steamboat Slough, I startle two mergansers, the first I've seen this season, and they fly off down the river, low over the water in typical merganser fashion. A little further on, I see a kingfisher fly off its perch on a low-hanging limb over the water, complaining that I have disturbed its fishing; that action is repeated by a second one a little further on. Probably because of the fog on my last row, I didn't see a single animal; it's good to see more action this time. There is a heron looking elegant over on the side of the river. Herons are the one large bird that stays around through the summer; I have been consistently sighting them flying across the river or perched along the bank, patiently waiting for a fish to swim near.

As I pass Eagle Tree on the way out, I see an eagle sitting in the sun on a high branch. This is the first eagle I have seen in over a month. It's my guess that the eagles have been away someplace where the salmon are plentiful. Maybe this guy is scouting the Snohomish and its tributaries to see if the salmon are back here yet. I had heard that they had opened fishing on the river for a couple of days on a couple of weekends because more Coho salmon were returning than had been expected. I have been expecting to see fishermen on the river, and seeing this eagle, I am now hoping what will attract the fishermen will bring back more eagles as the fall carries on.

In the last half mile before my turnaround, I encounter two deadheads that must have floated in since my last row. Some recent extra-high tides lifted them from where they were, and the strong accompanying currents placed them in their new locations, one right in mid channel. Avoiding these hazards, I reach Turnaround Tree and head back. It is easy to let a new obstacle drop from one's thoughts, particularly on the row home. I keep myself alert, manage with the help of my forward-view mirror to navigate around the two new deadheads, and then fall back into my almost automatic adjustments to those obstacles that have been in place for a while. As I pass Eagle Tree, I don't see the eagle that was there on my way down, but as I row on, it flies back in to take its place again on the same branch of the same tree.

A little breeze has come up during my time on the slough, and I have been noticing the varying effects of it and the current on my boat speed. The slowing effect of the head wind on my speed through the water was made worse when I was rowing with the current down the slough. On my return against the current, the wind helping me through the water feels stronger than it actually is. When I get into the river where the wind and current are running in the same direction, the wind will not affect my speed through the water as much.

Molly's Trail through the Ripples

I put my focus on my rowing and am soon at the head of Steamboat Slough and turn down the main river toward the dock. I am not surprised to see that, indeed, a number of outboard boats of various sizes have launched and are fishing on the river. With the help of my forward-view mirror, I am able to stay out of their way and make it back to the dock. The fishermen will be partners on the river for a while. I land, shoulder *Molly*, and head up the ramp. I can't help noticing that in contrast to the red alders, the leaves on that white alder that always welcomes me home at the top of the ramp still have a few more days in their summer green.

⅄⅄⅄

There is fog on the river again. The earth has radiated away its heat into the clear night sky, cooling the water vapor rising from the river and condensing it to fog. It is considerably foggier than it was the other day, but the water is calm, and as I bring *Molly* down to the dock, I can still see the other side of the river even now in the predawn light. It is quite cold—in the thirties—and I am wearing long pants and three upper layers for the first time this fall. I think this may be my last trip on the river in *Molly*. The tide is quite low and still going down, and I walk cautiously down the ramp; it is quite dark, and I want to avoid slipping on frost that I am guessing might have formed. All goes well, and I launch and am away. Oh, there is another sign of the season: my fingers are tingling with the cold.

It is still pretty dark when I make the turn down Steamboat Slough. Officially the sun has risen, and I can see it reflecting through the fog on the windows of some buildings across the river. However, it won't get over the Cascade Mountains far enough to light up the river area for a while. As I row down the slough, I see through the fog the dark, contorted shapes of the roots and stumps exposed along the banks by the low tide. It is quiet except for my breathing and the sound of my oars, and it feels a bit gloomy and mysterious. They are hard to make out, but there is a heron on the bank to my left and, a little further, another on a piling over on my right; both silently observe me pass.

The fog is pretty dense but fairly shallow; I can see the sky above. There are scattered thin clouds in the blue sky, now orange in this stage of the sun's rise. As I row down the slough and the sun rises more, those clouds turn white. The sun itself isn't yet visible, but I can now see it lighting up the tops of the trees. As I near my turnaround, I start to see its bright light in the fog behind the trees. It's not long

Sun's up on a Foggy Morning

before I begin to see the edge of the sun itself, and shortly after, the whole sun is visible.

Reaching Turnaround Tree, I head back. It's still foggy, and the lowering tide has me even deeper in the river channel, but the sunshine has fully invaded the scene, and that has given me more energy to put into my rowing. The herons I pass on the return—maybe the same ones I saw going out, maybe not—seem more animated as well. One of them manages to stay put as I pass, but the other flies off. I concentrate on my rowing, trying to keep my speed through the water over seven miles an hour. That brings me to the head of the slough, and I head downriver to the dock.

The sun has begun to warm up the air, and there is much less fog in the main river. The current helps me home, and it's not long before I row under the I-5 bridge. I do have to pull over to the side of the river; a couple of quads, two doubles, and a single shell from the Midmorning rowing group are assembled, waiting for their coach to lead them on their day's outing. I land, lift *Molly* onto my shoulders, and head toward the boathouse. There is a little frost on the dock, and I am glad for my caution during launch. I put *Molly* away and go home.

⅄⅄⅄

Between outings, I have switched my boats. I took *Molly* home and brought *Piper* down to my racks at the boathouse. Fall and winter weather brings more hazards to the river, and *Piper*'s greater stability and righting ability in the event of a capsize make her a good choice. I'm up early, eager to get out on the water on one of those few days without rain and wind that matches one of the opportunities on my calendar. Today, I am the only one at the boathouse. I had heard some gunfire yesterday, so I spend a few minutes before launching to again tape my air horn to the rigger so that I can let the hunters know that I am out there. The launch goes easily, and I am away.

The sun is not up, but there is enough light to see that it is cloudy with breaks in the lower clouds where the higher clouds are visible. An advantage of fall and winter rowing is the opportunity to experience the changing light of the sunrise. Right now the sky is a blue gray with just enough light to see the waves and swirls in the clouds. As I start to row, I see two otters swimming around in the water in the shadows along the east bank of the river. When they catch sight of me, they quickly disappear.

Another Sunrise over the Water

As I row up the river, I experience the beginnings of the sun's rise. The lower clouds remain gray, but where I can see through, the higher clouds now appear as islands of orange in that sea of gray. Just past the I-5 bridge, I encounter a number of seagulls sitting on the water together. At some point, each seagull dips its head and upper body under the water, pulls its head back up, and shakes the water off. They wait until the last minute to get out of my way and fly back to the same place when I get through. They seem to collect in the same place pretty regularly during the fall and winter months. I can only guess, but the Everett sewage treatment facility is nearby, and the treated water is released into the Snohomish River. The seagulls are there either because the treated water is warmer than what is flowing down the river, or something up the food chain from that effluent is an easy meal. A little into the row, I see one flock of Canada geese fly in formation across the river from east to west. Not far behind, another flock follows the same route. Happily, Canada geese are not among the hunters' targets. Another advantage of the later sunrise is the opportunity of catching river creatures as they start their day.

The shallow pond that runs along part of Steamboat Slough seems to be a favorite for duck hunters. I have been hearing a few gunshots, and I think that my general rule will be to stay in the main river for the rest of the season, particularly on weekends, when there is likely to be more hunters out, or when any degree of fog might hide my presence. I do like Steamboat Slough, where the scenery is more natural. I have never felt in danger during hunting seasons in the past, and my air horn does give me a way to let the hunters know that I am there. I think I will risk it.

The water is calm in the slough, and the evolving colors in the sky are reflecting in the water, distorted only by the waves from my boat and the disturbance created by the stroke of my oars. Not yet visible, the sun has risen to the point where those higher clouds have now turned white. And where it shines through under the cloud cover, there are splashes of orange in the gray. The appearance of the sun is also heating up the air, evaporating the clouds and revealing more and more blue sky.

Sunrise Reflecting on a Calm River

I have made it to the entrance of Ebey Slough, and since it is Sunday and I have all day, I decide to row up it a ways for a change of scenery. I concentrate on my rowing. I am pleased with the speed through the water that I am able to maintain today. Being shorter and wider than *Molly*, *Piper* is slower. However, in comparison to other rows in *Piper* from earlier this year, I am definitely able to maintain a faster speed. Part of it is probably the five pounds I have lost.

There is something swimming ahead of me. I can see it in my forward-view mirror. It sees me, and I hear a slap on the water and see it dive, most certainly a beaver. I've been seeing a number of ripple patterns in the water, and by the time I get there, whatever caused it—beaver, otter, or seal—is gone. I do see the occasional salmon swimming idly at the surface of the water with their dorsal fins exposed. They have been upstream and spawned, and the current has brought them down the river again. With their biological mission completed, they don't seem to care much about what happens to them, and I bump into a number of them as I row. It makes me wonder; with my two sons now grown and gone, maybe I, too, have completed my biological mission. Hopefully, there is some value in older humans for the survival of our species that the salmon doesn't have for its.

I make it to Five-Mile Bend, five miles along the shore from the dock, where my path makes a hard turn to the west, followed in short order with a turn back to the south. That's far enough—time to turn around and head back. The sun is now fully up, and it is still calm. The clouds have largely parted, and the reflection in the water of clouds and sky framed by that of the trees along the bank is inspiring. Every now and again, a very light breeze stirs the water, and the reflection starts to look like an impressionist painting.

As I row back down Ebey Slough, turn south into Steamboat Slough, and head for home, I look at the trees along the river. Some of the deciduous trees still cling to their now-dead leaves, appearing bright orange in the sun's light. Others, stripped of their leaves by the winds and rain of the last few weeks, stand with the complex architecture of their branches against the blue sky. On a high limb of one of these sits an eagle with its head and tail glowing white in the sunlight. It starts to take off and appears to get one of its talons stuck in the branch; it starts to fall upside down, but once loose from the branch, it rights itself in the air and flies back to land again on the tree.

Close to home, I see one lone Canada goose fly over the river behind me. A little later, another follows along. I imagine these guys got a late start and are racing to catch up with those flocks I saw leaving earlier. As I reach the dock and lift *Piper* onto my shoulders, a large flock of snow geese flies over high in the sky. They have arrived here from their summer habitat to winter in local fields. There is one large V formation with smaller ones on either side. As they fly along, one of the smaller Vs merges into the main formation. There are so many birds that I have *Piper* on its slings outside the boathouse before they are out of sight. It looks like I was the only rower out today. That's too bad; we may not have another day this nice this year.

⅄⅄⅄

It has been raining a lot. The TV meteorologist announced that we broke the record for rainfall for the month of October, over a half of foot more than normal, and it didn't slow down much in November and so far in December. Avoiding the rain and the wind that often come with it has kept me ashore, but I really want to get out. The forecast calls for a bit of a break this weekend, and I really want to get out on the water. Because it is Saturday and I have no place else I have to be all morning, I am going to wait until the sun is fully up to head out. When I arrive at the boathouse, I see the Saturday Masters Rowing Group readying their boats for an outing. It looks like a big group; I think others have felt themselves beached for too long. While I wait my turn, I watch the masters launch two eights and two quads and take off upriver. With the dock now clear, I launch *Piper* and head upriver far behind.

The occasional gunfire reminds me that it's hunting season and I need to stay in the main river. There is a strong current, and the push of the water through the river channel creates a disturbed flow that cause eddies to form. Moving through this water, the boat is pushed this way and that, and I have to row with a little anticipation to keep completely balanced. The river is brown with the dirt washed off the banks upriver, and there are also lots of sticks, branches, and the occasional log that the high water has washed into the river. I am glad I have my forward-view mirror. With its help, I am generally able to see what is washing toward me and get myself to the right or left to avoid trouble. However, I do keep hitting things, pieces of wood so waterlogged and floating so low that I don't see them. Fortunately, what I have been hitting is small, and it just bumps along on the boat, doing no harm.

Bypassing the entrance to Steamboat Slough, I see that the clouds to the east have lifted, revealing Three Fingers and Whitehorse Mountains. A little further on, at the Everett river harbor, I see that the cooler water has brought those big seals out of the water to spend some time on the log boom on the east side of the river. Over on the west side, some of commercial fishing vessels I hadn't seen for a while have been brought in to spend the winter alongside those here permanently in boat hospice.

Three Fingers and Whitehorse Mountains

Not far past the Highway 2 bridge, I see in my forward-view mirror that one of the masters quads has turned around and is heading my way. I pull far over to the right (my left) to get out of the way. The quad rows by, soon followed by the two eights and the other quad. The synchronized efforts of the rowers generate tremendous power, and the boats move off swiftly.

Now alone on the river, I turn my attention to the surroundings. Except for the blackberry bushes, all of the vegetation along the banks of the river has turned brown. The deciduous trees on both sides of the river have lost all their leaves; their complex branch work stands out sharply against the sky. In the fields to the east, the occasional cow watches me row by; to the west, the homeless camp has grown bigger than it was last winter. When the course of the river permits, I can see the very top of faraway Mount Baker. As I row, it appears to rise up from behind the nearby landscape.

A Masters Eight Rows By

Bare Tree against the Sky Reflecting in the Water

Cows Watch Me Row By

The current is strong, and I am rowing much further through the water than I am along the land. Progress is relatively slow, but I make it to the high-voltage power lines crossing the river. Two eagles sit on the top of one of the towers. It is not far from there to the sharp bend in the river at Lowell. The bend sends the water along in a series of eddies, requiring extra control on the oars. Continuing upriver, I hear the whistle blast and see a freight train travel through the Lowell community behind me. From there, it's a half mile along the land to my turnaround at the red farmhouse, almost a mile through the flowing water.

Red Farmhouse

The return trip downriver is going much quicker. At the end of my travel upriver, the Speed Coach reading of distance through the water was much higher than my GPS reading of distance along the land. Heading downriver, I can see the GPS reading catching up. On some outings, I will end up rowing further along the land than through the water, but that occurs only when the current changes direction or speed while I am out. Today there has been a strong downstream current, and the along-the-land mileage will get closer but will never catch the mileage through the water because I will have spent so much more time rowing slower upriver against the current than I will spend rowing downriver with it.

Not far along, I see a lone eagle in a high branch of one of the trees on the west side of the river. It stands out clearly, showing against the complex network of the tree's branches. I hear its peal call to me as I row by. Down at water level, three mergansers jump out of the water and fly downriver just above the surface. A little further downriver, a formation of large birds flies over. The high pitch of their honking and their extra-long necks make me think these are trumpeter or tundra swans here for the winter like the snow geese. They appear dark against the sky, but just as they pass over, their identity is confirmed when I see the white on their flapping wings.

I am feeling strong, rowing a good speed through the water, and aided by the current, I move quickly past Everett's river harbor and into the final stretch to the dock. This will be my last row of the year. Thinking about that reminds me of my last row of the year a couple of years ago. I had just arrived at Eagle Tree; no eagles were present. It was raining, and I had the hood of my jacket over my head, something I have not done since. The hood limited what I could see in my forward-view mirror. I strayed over too close to the shore, and my oar hit an old piling, and over I went. I had capsized a few times before but never that late in the year. The water was cold, but I was close enough to shore that I could stand up and quickly get myself back aboard. From there, I had to row back to the dock in December air temperature. The rowing kept my body core warm, but it was good to get into the shower to get some heat back into my lower legs and fingers. I am having no such trouble this year.

The current is still running downriver, but a moderate incoming tide has reduced its speed substantially, and the eddies have disappeared. It's cloudy but calm, and the river reflection is silver. As I near the end, a lone seagull flies over to my trail through the water, adjusts its course to mine, and, as did that seagull last summer, flies up over my head and away. Other birds have their seasons, but the seagulls are always here to share the river with me.

It's not long before I am back at the dock, and my rowing for the year is done. Walking up the ramp with *Piper* on my shoulders, I focus, as always, on the large again-leafless alder tree across the road, my Welcoming Tree. I think of the coming and going of its leaves that I observed over the course of the year.

I achieved my goal of rowing over a thousand miles. Actually, I rowed more miles this year than any year past. Looking ahead, I realize it's time to set that odometer in my head back to zero, and I wonder whether there will be another thousand miles in me next year. What gives me some confidence are what rowing gives me physically and mentally and what a great place the Snohomish River is in which to do it.

ABOUT THE AUTHOR

Raised in the Pacific Northwest, Bill Jaquette spent ten years in Missouri, first doing graduate work at the University of Missouri and then teaching philosophy at Southwest Missouri State University.

But his home was calling him, and he moved back to attend law school at the University of Washington. After attaining his law degree, Jaquette practiced for nearly forty years, spending much of that time as a public defender.

Jaquette began rowing on the Snohomish River after moving to Everett, Washington, where he held a position as director of the Snohomish County Public Defender Association. After a time, he joined the Everett Rowing Association. Keeping his shell in their boathouse, he was able to row much more frequently. Today, he rows two or three times a week, going eight to ten miles each outing.

Made in the USA
San Bernardino, CA
05 September 2017